# PEACE IS A FIRE

A Collection of Writings and Sayings

# PEACE IS A FIRE
## SANGHARAKSHITA

WINDHORSE PUBLICATIONS

Published by Windhorse Publications
Unit 1-316 The Custard Factory, Gibb Street, Birmingham, B9 4AA

© Sangharakshita, 1995
First published 1979
Second edition 1995

Printed by Biddles Ltd, Walnut Tree House,
Woodbridge Park, Guildford, GU1 1DA

Design: Dhammarati
Text compiled by Dharmachari Ananda
All photographs © the Clear Vision Trust Picture Archive

Cover: The Sun Setting among Dark Clouds
Courtesy of the Turner Collection, Tate Gallery, London

British Library Cataloguing in Publication Data:
A catalogue record for this book is available from the British Library.

ISBN 0 904766 84 5

# CONTENTS

# INTRODUCTION

In his essay 'Schopenhauer as Educator', Nietzsche refers to a traveller who, when asked on his return from extensive journeys what he had found common to all people, replied: 'They all tend to be inert.' This tendency, unfortunately, is still very much with us. How inspiring and invigorating it is to be prodded, if not blasted, out of this state of painful and apparently everlasting inertia and inner dullness! Such welcome displacement can be brought about by a scene of awe-inspiring beauty, an encounter with a place or person, in waking life or even in dream; or it might well be some phrase or passage in a book that jolts us out of our accustomed passivity. Words which have this power are those which not only penetrate our understanding, but also touch our feelings, so that we are able to apply what we read to our own experience, and our life is irrevocably affected.

There is a danger that this might be confused with what is commonly called 'having one's mind blown'. It seems that people are prepared to have their minds blown quite regularly, even twice a week, on the understanding that they can have their old minds back, completely intact, when the effects of the experience have died away, so long, that is, as there is the assurance of that blessed return to the norm, that is, inertia.

The experience I refer to, however, relates rather to something in the nature of 'religious' conversion, one which has the profound effect of changing the whole course of life, so that the old values are overthrown, our old minds uncomfortably dislodged, and we are henceforth all the time goaded out of inertia in the direction of our true creativity.

There is an urgent need, conscious or unconscious, among people today for anything which might awaken this creative potential. So it is a pleasure to have the opportunity to introduce this small volume, teeming with so much inspiring material.

Bearing in mind the author's maxim that one can generalize about people only to the extent that they are not individuals, it can be said that people often alternate between an unhealthy complacency which only perpetuates the general state of inertia referred to earlier, and a healthy unease about the basic existential situation. Vaguely irritated by such unease, I might open this book at the saying which informs me that 'there is never a state of equilibrium between the skilful and the unskilful.' This being so, I suddenly realize that in reality there is no such state as stagnation and that if I am not growing, I must be deteriorating! Thoughts like this can be not so much sobering as positively energizing, stimulating us out of our so-called complacency.

One of the attractions of a book of sayings and excerpts is that we can open it at random and have our interest immediately engaged, without feeling any need or obligation to read what comes immediately before or after. We are offered instead the rare treat of instant inspiration. Each individual saying speaks for itself. Yet the collection also provides a valuable introduction to the more extended writings of Sangharakshita.

Those who open the book in the expectation of being mainly entertained are sure to be disappointed, though there is a distinct flavour of the wit of Oscar Wilde in such aphorisms as:

*All art is (among other things) expression.*
*But not all expression is art.*

The breadth of Sangharakshita's thought is well represented in these pages, the sayings ranging from art in general and literature in particular, through sex and relationships, faith and morality, to philosophy and religion, especially Buddhism, with special emphasis on Buddhism as a means of development in the modern world. As for the depth of his thought, it is attested to by the crispness of his aphorisms. The aphorism as a literary form can so easily ring glib and hollow if it is not the fruit of long accurate observation and seasoned reflection.

One or two dominant themes emerge from this collection. One is the paramount need for us to break away from group conditioning, from superimposed customs and opinions, and become an individual. Another is the breach between thinking and feeling which becomes apparent soon after the initial breakaway from the group, a breach which is healed by increased awareness of our feelings, and by the development of positive emotions until thinking and feeling are completely integrated.

Though we might vainly hope that such integration will take place somehow miraculously or that 'someone without needs' will come along 'so that we can obtain from him everything for nothing', our deepest conscience tells us where the onus lies.

As Sangharakshita reminds us, 'we have a responsibility for our own growth, a responsibility for our own happiness.' May this inspired and inspiring book stimulate many readers into taking that responsibility.                    *Dharmachari Abhaya, 1978*

# SANGHARAKSHITA: *A Short Biography*

**P**ERHAPS THE FIRST THING that needs to be said about Sangharakshita is that he is an Englishman. He was born Dennis Lingwood in August 1925 and was brought up in Tooting, South London.

Suffering from a suspected heart condition, he was confined to bed for much of his early life. Unable to attend school, he took on the responsibility of educating himself and immersed himself in the classics of Western literature, ancient and modern.

It was when his grandfather showed him some objects brought from the Lama Temple in Beijing that Sangharakshita had his first encounter with Buddhism. From that moment he felt himself strongly drawn towards Eastern philosophy and art. Coming across Madame Blavatsky's *Isis Unveiled* at the age of fifteen, he suddenly saw that he was not a Christian – and never had been. He joined the London Buddhist Society and plunged into the study of Buddhist literature. It was after reading the *Sutra of Hui Neng* and the *Diamond Sutra* that he realized that what he was a Buddhist, and that he had always been.

In 1943, aged eighteen, Sangharakshita was passed as physically fit to be conscripted into the Army and sent to India with the Royal Corps of Signals. During the course of three years he had postings in India, Ceylon, and Singapore, where he made contact with several spiritual teachers and religious sects. He also began to write and give lectures on Buddhism, became a vegetarian, and took up the practice of meditation.

When the war came to an end he decided to stay on in India, with the aim of finding people who could show him how to follow the implications of the Buddha's teachings and live the life of a Buddhist. In the late 1940s, however, a Buddhist teacher of worth was rare indeed in a country from which Buddhism had been all but driven out more than seven hundred years before.

For several years Sangharakshita wandered from place to place on foot, meeting many of the teachers of the day. Most notably he spent time with Anandamayi, Ramdas, and Ramana Maharshi.

Gradually, Sangharakshita's aspiration to 'go for Refuge' (commit himself fully and effectively to Buddhism) became increasingly clear and he decided to seek ordination. In 1949 he received the lower ordination from the seniormost Theravadin monk in India and was given the name Sangharakshita, which means 'Protector of the Order'.

After receiving the higher ordination in 1950, and so becoming a fully ordained Buddhist monk, at the request of his teacher he moved to Kalimpong, a town on the border of India and Sikkim, not far from Tibet, where he stayed for fourteen years, studying, teaching, and writing. This period of his life is described in the volumes of his memoirs entitled *The Thousand-Petalled Lotus* and *Facing Mount Kanchenjunga*.

Perhaps the most important single work to emerge from that period was the book *A Survey of Buddhism*, published to world-wide acclaim in 1957. In the same year he established the Triyana Vardhana Vihara, a unique centre of interdenominational Buddhism.

Another crucial aspect of his work during this time was his involvement with the movement of mass conversion to Buddhism of ex-Untouchables started by Dr Ambedkar, the first Law Minister of independent India and the first 'Untouchable' ever to gain high office. The aim of the movement was to remove Untouchables from the horrific social and economic stigmas attached to their caste status by encouraging them to embrace Buddhism, so abandoning the Hindu system which had oppressed them and countless preceding generations.

With the Chinese invasion of Tibet, and the flood of refugees into India, Sangharakshita had the opportunity to meet many eminent lamas, in several cases developing close friendships. In 1962 he received the Bodhisattva precepts from Dhardo Rimpoche, thus adding Mahayana ordination to his existing Theravada ordination. He also received Vajrayana initiations from several of his Tibetan teachers.

In 1964 he was invited by the English Sangha Trust and the Buddhist Society to visit the UK. Sangharakshita came, realized the potential of Buddhism in this country, and decided to stay and work in the West. In 1967 he established the movement now known as the Friends of the Western Buddhist Order (FWBO), and a year later witnessed the 'Going for Refuge' of twelve men and women, thus initiating the Western Buddhist Order itself.

During the first few years of the FWBO's existence Sangharakshita maintained an intimate personal involvement with its activities, conducting meditation classes, leading retreats, and lecturing on all aspects of Buddhist teaching and tradition. Since then he has progressively handed over virtually all such day-to-day running of the FWBO to the Order.

In setting up the WBO, Sangharakshita felt particularly strongly that its members should not depend, as in the East, on charity, hence the emphasis on 'team-based Right Livelihood' businesses, which generate revenues as well as helping to cover the costs of running the FWBO centres. Equally importantly, they provide ethical forms of work for members of the Order and other Buddhists.

In the last ten years the most rapid development of the Movement has been in India. Even while fully involved with the creation of the FWBO and WBO, Sangharakshita never forgot his friends among the ex-Untouchables, and as soon as it was practicable he asked some of his Western disciples to go to India to continue the work he had started there. Since then many thousands have benefited from contact with the Indian wing of the FWBO, the Trailokya Bauddha Mahasangha Sahayak Gana.

Now based in London, Sangharakshita divides his time between writing, receiving visitors from within and outside the FWBO, and visiting the many new centres springing up all over the world.

THE SPIRITUAL PATH

*Buddhism and William Blake. Essay*

BUDDHISM IS A universal teaching. It speaks to all men. It speaks to them, moreover, not as belonging to any particular social group, e.g. clan, tribe, caste, race, nation, but as individual human beings. What it tells each one of them is that he can grow – that he can grow from manhood to Buddhahood, or from unenlightened humanity into enlightened humanity. It also tells him how he can do this.

*Aphorism*

Some are attracted to Buddhism because they find in it the confirmation of their ideas. It would be better if they were attracted by it because it refutes their ideas.

*Aphorism*

You cannot be a Buddhist unless you are free *not* to be a Buddhist. A Sinhalese, apparently, is not free not to be a Buddhist.

*A Method of Personal Development. Lecture*

One supremely important fact is that we *can* change; that consciousness *can* be restructured, *can* be redeveloped: hatred *can* be changed into love.

Buddhism is misunderstood if it is identified with just one or another of its specific forms, its particular cultural variants. It is rather like identifying a whole oak tree with just one single branch, or even, in some cases, with one single acorn.

*ibid.*

There is no such thing as natural man. Any attempt to treat man as other than a spiritual being distorts him.

*Aphorism*

Any kind of life which is making no effort to evolve is escapism.

*Aphorism*

What every living thing, what every living being, wants to do most of all is to fulfil the law of its own being, and the law of our being is – as it is the law of the being of every living thing – that we should develop.

*A Method of Personal Development. Lecture*

*A Method of Personal Development. Lecture*

How terrible it would be if in a year's time we were just the same people that we are today! And in five years' time, the same people! Ten years' time, or when we came to die!... None of us, surely, likes to think that even in a year's time – or maybe even next week, if we are sufficiently idealistic! – we'll be exactly where we are just at this moment.

*ibid.*

Buddhism is not yet really known in the West at all.

*The Three Jewels*

In reality Buddhism is neither pessimistic nor optimistic. If compelled to label it in this way at all we should borrow a word from George Eliot and call it melioristic, for though asserting that conditioned existence is suffering it also maintains, as the Third Aryan Truth teaches, that suffering can be transcended.

# THE VOICE OF SILENCE

Close, eyes; behold no more the rich array
Of forms and vivid colours. Touch, be still;
Grope not for lover's hand, or lips that will
Sting you awake to bliss by night or day.
Relish no more the scent of new-mown hay,
Or flowers, or incense, nostrils. Take your fill
Of tastes no more, O watery tongue, nor trill
Delicious notes in cadence grave or gay.

For when the senses and the sensual mind
Are laid asleep, and self itself suspended,
And naught is left to strive for or to seek,
Then, to the inmost spirit, thrice refined,
Thrice pure, before that trance sublime has ended,
With voice of thunder, will the Silence speak.

# SUFFERING
## AND HAPPINESS

*Aphorism*  IF ONE IS UNHAPPY, one wants to know the reason why. But it never occurs to one to ask why one is happy. It is therefore unhappiness, rather than happiness, that causes us to reflect upon our condition. It is unhappiness that makes us think.

*Seminar on The Precious Garland*  The tragedy is not that we don't get what we want, but that we *do* get what we want, and then we're stuck with it, and very often we find that it's not what we wanted at all.

*The Three Jewels*  What the third *lakshana*[1] really means is, in positive terms, that nirvana alone is peace, and negatively that conditioned things are painful because we seek in them for that absolute bliss which only the Unconditioned can bestow and have, therefore, inevitably to experience disappointment and frustration.

*The Path of the Inner Life*  Mankind progresses for the same reason that the amoeba evolves – from irritation. There was never any flower of human achievement but some great sorrow lay at its root.

Sometimes, of course, we just try – we may even do our best – to forget the whole bothersome question of personal development. Especially when it's a fine summer day, and the beach is calling, and your friends, maybe, want to take you out, you think: 'Why bother? Why not just be an ordinary human being and forget all about this question of the Higher Evolution and Personal Development?' But, fortunately or unfortunately, luckily or unluckily, once you've reached a certain point, once self-consciousness has really started to emerge, once you've really started to think, once you've really started to *feel*, once you've really started to *imagine*, you cannot really do that.

*A Method of Personal Development. Lecture*

The happiness that you feel when you satisfy a desire is not due to the satisfaction of the desire but to the momentary cessation of the desire. But the desire returns. Therefore desires can never be satisfied: they can only be overcome, abandoned.

*Seminar on The Door of Liberation*

*The Stages of the
Spiritual Path.
Lecture*

This is what is really meant by *duhkha*: a sort of disharmony, a jarring quality that we experience in the course of our everyday life in this world.… Things are never one hundred per cent right. There's always something, even if it's a little something, that goes wrong. Even in the course of the most beautiful day it seems, only too often, a cloud has to float across the face of the sky. Something goes wrong. Maybe you've prepared expectantly for a very beautiful day. You're going to meet somebody whom you like, things are going to be so lovely, so beautiful. But then some absurd incident happens and it all goes wrong. Then you feel completely out of tune, completely 'jangled', by whatever has happened. And very often this is our experience of life. Most of the time this is how we go through life, feeling like this. We find that everything from which we expected so much fails and doesn't live up to our expectations. This sort of experience is what is called *dukhka*, Unsatisfactoriness or Suffering.

We have a responsibility for our own life, a responsibility for our own growth, a responsibility for our own happiness.

*A Method of Personal Development. Lecture*

Happy is the man whose needs and whose wants coincide.

*Aphorism*

Experiences are rarely satisfying in themselves: only in anticipation and recollection.

*Seminar on The Door of Liberation*

People who suffer are not necessarily nearer to the realization of the Aryan Truth of Suffering than those who do not. One can, indeed, have insight into the Truth of Suffering while experiencing happiness (e.g. when meditating), for in the transcendental perspective even happiness is suffering – not in the sense of being actually painful, as a sensation or a feeling, but in the sense of being a conditioned thing.

*Correspondence*

RELIGION & BELIEF

*Aphorism*  IT IS BEST NOT TO BELIEVE in God. If one does believe in him, one should at least disobey him. To believe in him *and* obey him is pitiable.

*Aphorism*  We ceased to believe in God the day he was proved to exist.

*Aphorism*  The meaning of life is to be found only beyond life.

*Aphorism*  Ultimate spiritual choices are not to be determined by cultural considerations.

*Aphorism*  Religions, as they have come down to us, are gold mixed with ore. Sometimes the quantity of gold is so small, compared with the quantity of ore, that it is not worth the labour of extraction. Better open up a new mine.

*Aphorism*  An ethnic religion is one whose members have a common past; a missionary religion, one in which they have a common future.

Religions that have gone rotten with age are good for compost, not food.

*Aphorism*

Better to end up on the dung heap than in a museum.

*Aphorism*

If Christianity is of supernatural origin, I fail to see how it can be 'part' of our cultural heritage. One is therefore not being untrue to the heritage if one rejects Christianity.

*Aphorism*

Religion is essentially the experience of egolessness; the truly religious life is the life of egolessness; and genuinely religious beliefs and practices are those by which the realization of egolessness can be achieved.

*The Religion of Art*

The besetting sin of organized Christianity is intolerance, that of Islam fanaticism, of Hinduism inhumanity, and of Buddhism laziness and indifference.

*Aphorism*

Universalism does not mean comparing the letters of different traditions, but trying to get through to the spirit.

*Aphorism*

*Seminar on Outlines of Mahayana Buddhism*

I think it is, in a way, very suspect (to say) that there is a separate religious sense, or a separate religious consciousness, and that some people have it and some people don't.… If you use the word religious it seems to indicate a sort of co-ordination of all one's faculties and one's whole being in a certain direction which you recognize to be ultimate.

*ibid.*

It seems to me that if you use the words 'religious consciousness', it's a total consciousness. It's when all of your being – your head and your heart and your will – is directed, totally and integrally if possible, on to those things or that thing which you regard as of the highest importance and significance: then you can speak in terms of the 'religious consciousness'. It's not a sort of separate faculty, which needs a separate satisfaction. It's your own total commitment to, or total preoccupation with, what is, as far as you can see, of absolute importance – or of the greatest importance, if you like. It's not a *separate kind* of consciousness.

In a traditional civilization ... religion (to use the narrow modern term) is not something from which a man can escape, even if he wants to; for it encounters him at every step, with the familiar objects of home and the accustomed routine of daily life. Nurtured in such an environment, in which the whole of existence appears to be a great Smaragdine Tablet, constantly reminding us that 'the things below are copies' and that the originals are above, sensitive hearts and minds become more subtle and sensitive still. To them 'rocks, and stones, and trees', and other natural objects, are not simply lumps of matter of various shapes and sizes, but 'huge cloudy symbols of a high romance' traced, not by the 'magic hand of chance', but by the irresistible finger of omnipresent spiritual law. Nature is not dead, but alive with many voices, and to an eye accustomed to see and to hear things that point beyond themselves, even

*An old pine tree is preaching wisdom,*
*And a wild bird crying out truth.*

*A Survey of Buddhism*

To be a pagan is to have a positive attitude towards Nature and towards oneself as a part of Nature.

*Aphorism*

WORK AND ACTION

*Aphorism*   OUTER ACHIEVEMENTS should be expressions of inner abundance, not compensation for inner poverty.

*Aphorism*   People who have no real work of their own to do will always interfere with that of others. They may even make it their 'work' to interfere.

*Aphorism*   Find the truth, and then live by it.

*Aphorism*   'Work makes the companion,' says Goethe. Therefore, if you have no work you have no companion. Those are not companions with whom we merely amuse ourselves.

*Aphorism*   That one is able to do a thing is no reason for doing it.

*Aphorism*   There is no such thing as the will. What we think of as the will is simply our idea of ourselves as performing an action. To say that we *will* to do something is meaningless. We do it – or do not do it. The will is a myth.

One should be useful – but useful only within the much larger context of complete uselessness.

*Seminar on the Ratnaguna-Samchayagatha*

One should try to be too big to be used.

*ibid.*

It's a virtue to be ornamental as well as useful.

*ibid.*

Success in any field is not without its drawbacks.

*Correspondence*

I sometimes quite happily do nothing! But when I'm doing nothing, I don't mean 'not doing anything'! Not sort of sitting there in a slightly negative mood feeling that you're not doing anything but maybe you ought to be doing something. If there is something to be done, well, of course, do it! But if there is nothing to be done, well, *positively enjoy* that state of not doing anything!

*Seminar on The Buddha*

To be able to do one thing at a time is the whole art of life.

*Aphorism*

*Seminar on The Door of Liberation*  It is not a sign of spirituality to allow oneself to be exploited. Sooner or later you begin to start resenting it.

*Seminar on The Door of Liberation*  You can't help helping others when you are truly helping yourself.... One can help others even simply by providing facilities whereby they can help themselves. The importance of being able to help others in a supportive way is also very great. In a way, even people in the forefront of our activities are only supporting the whole activity of the Sangha. This is developing the faculty of rejoicing in merit.

*Aphorism*  We should consider, not so much how our actions stand in relation to one another, as how they stand in relation to Reality.

*Correspondence*  Surely we are very near to heaven, if not to nirvana, if we enjoy our work, and if our work is our life!

You learn what it is that you are trying to do in the process of trying to do it.

A Method of Personal Development. Lecture

Correspondence

The deeper the internal realization, the broader and stronger should be the outflow of energy. A spirituality that is sterile in respect of 'good works' is highly suspect. Of course, there is such a thing as purely spiritual action on higher levels of consciousness, and this is far more effective than ordinary action, but for most treaders of the spiritual path it is many, many years before this stage is reached, and meanwhile we have to busy ourselves with humble, everyday tasks of service on the mundane level.

Unless your work is your meditation, your meditation is not meditation.

Aphorism

It is wrong to distinguish between what a man is and what he does. There are no mute inglorious Miltons. If he is mute he is not Milton. That one does *not* do something is part of one's character.

Aphorism

*Aphorism*   A skilful act is one which is an expression of will-to-growth rather than neurotic need, which is emotionally positive, which is an act of the total individual, and which is orientated towards a higher state of being.

*Aphorism*   The true revolutionary does not play other people's games – including the game of violence.

*Aphorism*   In the minds of those who prefer evolution to revolution there is always a conflict between loyalty to the past and loyalty to the future.

*Aphorism*   When the old order dies, two possibilities reveal themselves: one, that the old order shall be restored under a new name; two, that a genuinely new order shall come into existence. At the beginning, it is very difficult to distinguish between the two.

*Aphorism*   If one does not dream, one becomes a monster.

Some say they experience the will as 'free'. But one who experiences it as free and one who experiences it as unfree, as determined, have in fact the same experience. Both have the experience of *acting*. On this experience they superimpose the ideas – not to say the fictions – of freedom and bondage.

*Aphorism*

Perfect work comes from the unification of pure wisdom and pure deeds.

*Seminar on The Door of Liberation*

Most of our friends find that they need to alternate between exertion and relaxation, work and meditation. Eventually the two must become one, or rather must interfuse, the one not getting in the way of the other. Meanwhile, we need to pursue both, at different times. Both are necessary to our spiritual development.

*Correspondence*

*Aphorism*

WHILE OTHER PEOPLE are busy making up our minds for us in small matters, we are at liberty to make up our own in great.

*The Stages of the Spiritual Path. Lecture*

Nowadays there's quite a lot of talk about freedom, and most people, it seems, think that freedom means simply doing what one likes. But the Buddhist conception of freedom is rather different.... In the first place it's … complete freedom from all subjective emotional and psychological bias, complete freedom from prejudice, from all psychological conditioning. Secondly [it is] freedom from all wrong views, all ignorance, all false philosophy and mere opinion. It is this sort of freedom, this total spiritual freedom – freedom of heart and mind, at the highest possible level, at the summit of one's existence – which is the aim and object of Buddhism.

*Aphorism*

The fact that the second precept[2] is worded in terms of 'not taking the not-given' suggests that, ethically speaking, there is no such thing as rights. All rights are based upon power, i.e. on capacity to exert force.

Buddhism, properly and deeply understood, and
thoroughly and extensively applied, is *revolutionary*. It
is revolutionary, that is to say, within the context of the
established order. It is in this realization that our
breakthrough consists: in the realization of the fact that
Buddhism has to transform every aspect of our lives and
be not just something that we theoretically understand,
not just a little hobby with which we occupy ourselves
once or twice a week, but the transforming agent, the
transforming influence – the catalyst, if you like – of our
lives.

*Breaking Through into Buddhahood. Lecture*

Awareness is revolutionary.

*Aphorism*

In what does the extension of the FWBO consist? Not in
the publicizing of a personality, not in the popularization
of an idea, but in the growth of a new society and a new
world.

*Aphorism*

*Aphorism*   Negative emotions are much stronger in man than positive emotions. Any individual or organization that wants to influence or control people in large numbers, in the mass, therefore does so by manipulating their negative emotions. The Catholic Church plays upon fear, the Communist Party on hate, Capitalism on greed, totalitarian states on feelings of inadequacy and inferiority. One may also say that in time of peace the state plays more on people's greed, in time of war more on their fear.

*Aphorism*   A state is governed by a combination of force and inertia – force, on the part of the minority; inertia, on the part of the majority.

*Aphorism*   Tradition was once innovation; what is now innovation may one day be tradition.

*A System of Meditation. Lecture*   Your power should be the function of your being.

## STANZAS

'Hammer your thoughts into a unity.'
This line once read
The sound came clangingly
Of golden hammers in my head
Beating and beating sheet on sheet
To make the figured foil complete.

Religion, friendship, art
Were hammered there
On the cyclopean anvils of my heart
Into an image bright and fair.
Under the strain the forge-floor split;
Nerveless the arms that fashioned it.

# FOURTH METAMORPHOSIS

Too long have I been a camel
Ship of the Desert
Too long knelt to be laden
With other men's merchandise.

Too long have I been a lion
Lord of the Jungle
Too long fought
Paper-and-tinsel dragons

Too long have I been a child
Parent of the Future

Now it is time to be
Myself.

# DREAM

Nightrace of silver-white coach of ghostly
Sledge maybe chariot drawn
By white horses, nightrace
Through whitewinter landscape through frozen-
Fast-world. In the back, behind me, –
Arms slightly spread, rime-bright hair
Stiff on your shoulders, palms
Open, cold blue eyes staring, – you
Silverking deadking driving
Towards Spring towards Winter
Who knows.

THE ARTS

*The Religion of Art*  ART IS THE ORGANIZATION of sensuous impressions into pleasurable formal relations that express the artist's sensibility and communicate to his audience a sense of values that can transform their lives.

*The Path of the Inner Life*  It has been recognized even in the West (by Schopenhauer) that all great Art contains an element of self-transcendence akin to that which constitutes the quintessence of religion. When this element of self-transcendence is consciously cultivated in poetry, in music, or in painting and sculpture, instead of the element of mere sensuous appeal, Art ceases to be a form of sensuous indulgence and becomes a kind of spiritual discipline, and the highest stages of aesthetic contemplation become spiritual experiences.

*Art and Spiritual Life. Lecture*  One cannot be an artist without at the same time participating in the Higher Evolution.

*Aphorism*  All art is (among other things) expression. But not all expression is art.

When we experience a work of art we momentarily experience the same state of mind that the artist experienced when he created that work. Thus ... the artist contributes to the Higher Evolution of other people and of the race.

*Art and Spiritual Life. Lecture*

Perhaps only in the field of poetry have the English been truly great.

*Aphorism*

Coleridge, as a thinker, was a sublime abortion. He had greater mental endowment than any Englishman perhaps ever had, and he would have been one of the greatest religious thinkers of all time. But he was severely hampered, crippled even, by his attachment to orthodox Christianity. His inability to reconcile the Trinitarian Christian in him with his own true, original genius was the cause, not the effect, of his famous indolence.

*Aphorism*

Coleridge was the greatest thinker the English have produced, only his Christianity did not allow him to think.

*Aphorism*

*Aphorism*   D.H. Lawrence's writings are not works of art, but the works of an artist. When he does achieve a 'work of art', therefore, it seems both natural and miraculous.

*Aphorism*   *Commentaries on Living*, by J. Krishnamurti – the title gives the whole show away completely.

*Aphorism*   Milton's *Paradise Lost* is an imaginative statement of the whole dilemma of modern man.

*Aphorism*   *Paradise Lost* has claim to be considered the most important work in English literature.

*Aphorism*   If you are looking for evidence of rebirth, listen to Mozart's Symphony No. 1 – composed at the age of eight.

*Aphorism*   Beethoven at his worst – and perhaps at his most characteristic and popular – is will pretending to be power.

The myth of Perseus and Medusa: he could cut off her head only by looking at it not directly, which would have petrified him, but indirectly, at the reflection in his shield. Similarly we cannot confront reality, especially our own psychic reality, directly: it would kill us. Art, etc. is the medium.

*Aphorism*

The spiritual aspirant is like Shelley's Skylark: while his understanding soars, his emotions sing. It is in this singing and soaring, in the simultaneous expansion of the understanding and the emotions, that we find the meaning of Buddhism and the value of art, and, in fact, the secret of spiritual life.

*Buddhism and Art*

The more creative someone is the less predictable he is.

*Seminar on the Ratnaguna-Samchayagatha*

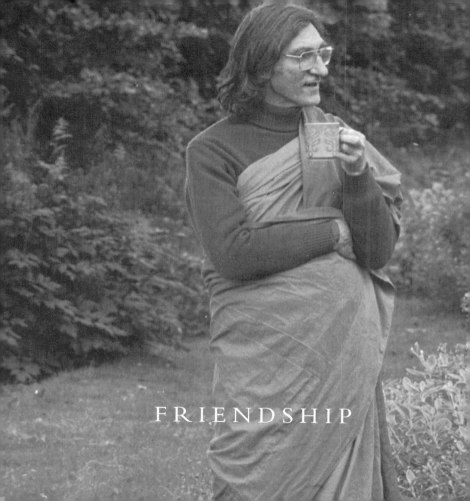

FRIENDSHIP

*Correspondence*

VERY FEW PEOPLE KNOW the real meaning of friendship. More often than not, there is too much emphasis on sentiment, and too little on action. *Metta* is something that must be *lived*.

*A System of Meditation. Lecture*

We should have strong feelings of *metta* towards our own self – don't forget that! – and towards others, strong feelings of spiritual fellowship. And when I say 'strong feelings' I mean *strong* feelings, not something tepid and lukewarm and half-hearted and faint-hearted, but really warm; even, if you like, a little hot! And strong, not feeble.

*Correspondence*

Paradoxical though it may seem, being less concerned with oneself (in the selfish sense) and loving oneself (in the sense of directing *metta* to oneself) are not incompatible. It is, in fact, the person who does not truly love himself who is concerned with himself in an egocentric, even a neurotic, sort of way.

The cynic feels less than is justified; the sentimentalist more than is justified.

*Seminar on Dhyana for Beginners*

Only individuals can practise true friendliness.

*ibid.*

It is impossible for people to live together without mutual forgiveness.

*Aphorism*

Have sympathy for those who are going through a difficult phase – nearly everybody goes through it some time or another: if not this year, next year; if not this week, next week. Some of you, I know very well, were going through it last week – not to say the day before yesterday! We know this! Everybody has his turn. Everybody has a difficult phase to go through occasionally. So if you yourself are not going through a difficult phase, and somebody else is, be sympathetic – I mean, wisely sympathetic, not indulgent. Don't use the occasion as an opportunity for asserting your own relative, temporary superiority to that sort of thing.

*A System of Meditation. Lecture*

*Seminar on The Stability of Societies*

I think one should distinguish between: (1) neurotic craving for company as a means of escape from your own inner emptiness; (2) a healthy human desire for human contact; (3) a wish, or aspiration, for spiritual fellowship. We should have nothing to do with the first stage, a modest place for the second, and develop the third as much as we can.

*ibid.*

You must not relate to a neurotic person on the basis of his neurosis.

*A System of Meditation. Lecture*

Speaking in an ordinary sort of way – leaving aside transcendental things – positive emotion is the life-blood of the Order. If there's no positive emotion in the Order, there is no life in it at all, and no life, therefore, in the Movement. So the development of positive emotion in each one of us and in all of us in association with one another is absolutely crucial.

*Seminar on The Buddha*

Unless you are a healthy, growing individual – unless, as it were, you love yourself – you can't love others.

If a normal, healthy person loses someone who is near and dear to him, this is not neurotic suffering, this is real suffering.... And one can genuinely and wholeheartedly sympathize with that person, and know that he will get over it in due course, because he is healthy. In a healthy person, there might be a slight element of neurosis, but nothing to speak of, as it were. In such a case, you know that time will heal the wound. Neurosis is not healed by time.

*Seminar on The Stability of Societies*

'What do you do for a living?' I asked. His hand shook so badly, as he lit another cigarette, that he knocked over the whisky bottle at his elbow. 'Oh, I'm a psychiatrist,' he said. 'I help people who have problems.'

*Aphorism*

We are not kept going by abstract ideas, we are kept going by our emotions. It is our positive emotions which keep us going on the spiritual Path – which give us inspiration, enthusiasm and so on – until such time as we can develop Perfect Wisdom and be motivated by that.

*A System of Meditation. Lecture*

*A Method of Personal Development. Lecture*

If you are not happy with yourself, if you are not at ease with yourself, if you don't like yourself – and many people nowadays, unfortunately, don't like themselves – you can't like other people. Your so-called liking of other people mustn't be what Nietzsche called 'your bad love of yourself', by which he meant your disliking of yourself.

*ibid.*

I'd even go so far as to say that without strong positive emotion, no spiritual progress is possible. I'd even put it as strongly as that. This means that many people's first duty to themselves and to others is simply to be happy: to develop friendliness, compassion, sympathetic joy, equanimity, and reverence and devotion.

*Correspondence*

It is hardly possible to have a neutral attitude towards [parents], I think, which means that if one's attitude is not positive it is negative, and if one's attitude to those who are so closely connected with one as one's parents are is negative it is likely to have a deleterious effect on one's whole attitude towards life, including other people.

*The Four Limitless States.*[3] *Metta* is the basis of them all. When our friendliness comes into contact with suffering, compassion arises. When our friendliness comes into contact with other people's happiness, sympathetic joy arises. When friendliness, compassion, and sympathetic joy are developed equally towards all, then equanimity arises. Equanimity is not indifference; there's no equanimity without friendliness. We can also add reverence or devotion. This is experienced when the *metta*, the friendliness, is directed as it were upwards towards the ideal, the spiritual ideal.

*A Method of Personal Development. Lecture*

It is absolutely wrong to say that by 'isolating' oneself from the opposite sex in single-sex communities one loses the opportunity of contacting the 'other side' of one's nature, which the other sex symbolizes. The precise opposite is the case. In single-sex communities men and women tend to develop, and integrate into their own spiritual life and practice, the 'feminine' and 'masculine' qualities which are normally projected on to the opposite sex and which normally *stay projected*.

*Correspondence*

*Correspondence*  As for friendship, it is probably true that you have never – or only very fleetingly – experienced the nature of real friendship, and have never been anyone's friend. *Real friendship is very rare indeed*, and if you haven't experienced it, neither have a lot of other people, including many who would like to think they have. The fact that real friendship is so rare should not make us cynical, of course, but only more determined to develop real friendship, and be a real friend, ourselves, and the first step towards developing a quality is realizing that we don't have it.

*ibid.*  More and more I think that communication cannot be hurried, and that friendship needs time and patience for its development.

*ibid.*  Having once met, we can never really be separated, even though we may be physically apart, and though no spoken or written word may pass between us for a long time.

Getting truly to know another human being is like
exploring a new continent – or another world. One
plunges into abysses, wanders among lofty mountains, is
lost in the depths of mysterious forests, rests in bowers
of roses with the brook sparkling beside one and the
birds singing in the branches overhead, and stands on
lonely shores gazing out over the illimitable expanse of
sunlit waters.

*Aphorism*

Unless one has lived completely alone for a while one
hardly knows what life is all about – certainly unless one
is able to live alone one is not really able to live with
other people.

*Correspondence*

It is not enough to sympathize with something to such
an extent that one agrees with it. If necessary, one must
sympathize to such an extent that one disagrees.

*Aphorism*

Angels are to men as men are to women – because they
are more human and, therefore, more divine.

*Aphorism*

*Correspondence*    The best relationships ... are surely those which are based on sincerity and straightforwardness, on mutual trust and confidence, which grow stronger and more satisfying with the years, and into which the element of game-playing never enters.

*ibid.*    So long as you are aiming at Enlightenment, you will be relating, directly or indirectly, to everybody else who is aiming at Enlightenment, and that is the only form of relating that really matters.

*ibid.*    In the FWBO we do not have a puritanical attitude towards sex, but at the same time it must be recognized that it belongs to the lower, not to the Higher, evolution of man, and that its place is at the periphery rather than at the centre of our existence. Nowadays people tend to 'over-invest' in the sexual-romantic type of relationship, with the result that their emotional balance is constantly being threatened and peace of mind becomes impossible of achievement. So long as this state of affairs continues, no real spiritual progress is possible.

Positive human relationships have their own value, but a *spiritual* relationship, i.e. a relationship based on the effective pursuit of a common spiritual ideal – in our case the ideal of Enlightenment – is an entirely different matter, and the one must never be mistaken for the other.

*ibid.*

So far as I can see, the 'woman question' is a difficulty only to the extent that men are weak, i.e. are emotionally dependent on women. If men are 'strong', i.e. are not emotionally dependent in this manner, then they can provide women with the kind of support that most of them seem to need, as well as get on with the task of their own spiritual development. Paradoxically, a woman can really rely on a man only if he is committed to something that is more important to him than she is. If she is the most important thing in his life, then heaven help her – and him.

*ibid.*

To a man, celibacy means that he is deprived of sex; to a woman, that she is not wanted.

*Aphorism*

*Correspondence*  Between male and female there will always be war, or at least tension. The only solution is for both men and women to try to develop both 'masculine' and 'feminine' qualities within themselves and relate to one another as individuals. This may well involve the separation of the sexes, so that neither is tempted to project on to the other the qualities which it lacks.

*ibid.*  Whether in the case of men or women, I am not convinced by the argument that one needs sex in order to keep in touch with one's emotions. It is true that sex does give one, momentarily, a feeling of warmth towards others, but this is really no more than the 'good mood' into which any kind of sense satisfaction is able to put one. It bears no resemblance to the experience of *metta*, which takes place on quite another level, and it is a great mistake to confuse the two, or to think that the one brings one any nearer to the other.

*Aphorism*  To the extent that one is dominated by the sex-instinct one is not an individual.

In the case of a mentally healthy person his or her
principal support is always within, so that even when,
owing to changed circumstances, external supports in
the form of personal relationships are no longer there, he
or she is able to go on functioning as before with little or
no difficulty.

*Correspondence*

A married man is like a donkey tethered to a post: within
a restricted area he can move about as he wishes. An
unmarried man, who carries on a succession of 'affairs',
is like a convict carrying a ball and chain: he is free to
go wherever he pleases, but he has to carry with him the
iron ball, and this is so heavy that every now and then he
has to stop and rest, temporarily immobilized.

*Aphorism*

Any normal person ought to be able to live alone.

*Seminar on The
Door of Liberation*

*Seminar on The Stability of Societies*

You can't really live with other people unless you can live without them. If you're happy on your own, you can be happy with others. If you can't be happy on your own, you can't be happy with others. In that case you're with them, not because you want to be with them, but because you don't want to be on your own. Your being with them isn't a real being with them. It isn't positive. It is only an escape from yourself.

*Seminar on the Sutta-Nipata*

There is not much point in giving up sex as a sort of discipline when the neurotic craving and dependence is still there, and maybe finding outlets in other ways. You may be still just as neurotically attached to your dog or cat.

*ibid.*

I sometimes say that there are two kinds of sexuality: neurotic and non-neurotic. The non-neurotic is when there is sexual activity, not through any need for security – for example, through sex, or through the 'relationship' – but just because you are young and healthy. Neurotic sexuality is where there is not only the actual sexual urge, but also an infantile craving for security, contact, warmth, and so on, through sexual relationship or activity. It may be, in the case of some people, that they do experience higher states of consciousness … yet at the same time a certain amount of sexual activity may go on, but this will certainly be non-neurotic. However,… the great test is how you feel if the relationship breaks up. If your partner, or lover, or whatever, says 'Bye-bye! I've found someone else,' if you can say 'That's great! See you some time,' and just accept it happily, then you had no neurotic craving along with your sexual relationship and activity. But if you are 'cut up', upset, and disturbed, and can't meditate for months, well, obviously there has been a strong neurotic element. So that is the criterion,… whether one can remain happy whatever happens, whatever storms may come.

# LIFE IS KING

Hour after hour, day
After day we try
To grasp the Ungraspable, pinpoint
The Unpredictable. Flowers
Wither when touched, ice
Suddenly cracks beneath our feet. Vainly
We try to track birdflight through the sky trace
Dumb fish through deep water, try
To anticipate the earned smile the soft
Reward, even
Try to grasp our own lives. But Life
Slips through our fingers
Like snow. Life
Cannot belong to us. We
Belong to Life. Life
Is King.

## AT THE BARBER'S

Talkative one morning, the Cypriot barber
Asked me what I did for a living.
'Write', I replied, not feeling
Particularly communicative. 'You write!
What do you write?' 'I write poetry.'

Ah, delight of the suspended scissors, exhilaration
Of the raised comb! 'You write
*Poetry!*'
　　　　　In depths of the mirror behind him
Athenian walls standing intact,
Long-haired warriors spared for great verses.

THE SPIRITUAL COMMUNITY

*Aphorism*    A GROUP IS UNITED by its lowest common denominator, a spiritual community by its highest common factor.

*Aphorism*    An orchestra is a spiritual community – at least while it is playing.

*Aphorism*    The relation between the individual and the 'positive community' should be like that between soloist and orchestra in a concerto.

*Seminar on The Precious Garland*    Lay life may be said to be any situation which prevents one's higher development. This may occur even within the context of a formally monastic situation.

*Seminar on The Door of Liberation*    In a spiritual movement you can have a teacher but you can't have a leader.

*Aphorism*    One should try to avoid close association *only* with those with whom one feels close affinities: one should attempt to go beyond this level – this affords great opportunities to see one's own reactions at work.

Despite their different life-styles, Order members in particular should be able to relate to one another in a thoroughly positive manner, on the basis of their common commitment to the Three Jewels[4] – a commitment which far transcends all social differences.

*Correspondence*

You can't really commit yourself to something that you know. To commit yourself to the known is a contradiction in terms. You always commit yourself to the unknown. At least there is always an unknown element in that to which you commit yourself.

*Seminar on the Ratnaguna-Samchayagatha*

If you have seen through something, you're no longer involved in it. You withdraw from it. It's just like seeing a mirage in a desert. At first we may be very interested in those palm trees and that apparent oasis, and we may be hastening in that direction. But as soon as we see that it's a *fata morgana*, and isn't really there, then we're no longer really interested. We stop, and don't hasten in that direction any longer.

*The Stages of the Spiritual Path. Lecture*

*The Path of Regular and the Path of Irregular Steps. Lecture*

We speak of lay ordination, monastic ordination, and even Bodhisattva[5] ordination, but all three are ordinations: the same word, *samvara*,[6] is applied to each and every one of them, upasaka,[7] bhikshu,[8] and Bodhisattva all equally going for Refuge. The upasaka goes for Refuge, the bhikshu goes for Refuge, and the Bodhisattva, perhaps in a higher and deeper sense still, goes for Refuge: all three commit themselves. Any difference between them is simply as regards the number, and in the case of the Bodhisattva, the kind, of precepts observed. So that what the monk and the layman, the bhikshu and the upasaka, have in common, is far more important than what they do not have in common. What they have in common is the three Refuges.[9] And nothing can be more important for the Buddhist than that.

*ibid.*

This is the root, this is the foundation, this is the absolute bedrock of our spiritual life; this is how we really start practising the Path – by Going for Refuge.

*Question:* Can a mitra[10] who joins in with the chanting    *Aphorism*
of the Refuges and Precepts, be said to go for Refuge,
even though he is not an *upasaka*?[7]
*Answer:* There is no question of an absolute difference,
as between light and darkness, between one who has
gone for Refuge and one who has not. Intermediate
degrees exist. Even if one merely thinks about going for
Refuge – even merely hears about it – to an infinitesimal
degree one has gone for Refuge.

Honest collision is better than dishonest collusion.    *Aphorism*

# MORALITY

*Aphorism*   IF VALUES DO NOT EXIST one must create them. Otherwise one cannot evolve.

*Aphorism*   Hitler's killing the Jews was an evil action; but it was evil because they were human beings, not because they were Jews.

*Aphorism*   It is easy to forgive people their vices. What is sometimes more difficult is to forgive them their virtues.

*Aphorism*   One stone divides the whole stream.

*Aphorism*   For 'confession' to be possible, there should be no feeling of guilt.

*Seminar on The Door of Liberation*   It is the spirit of renunciation which renders fruitful all one's religious observances.

*Aphorism*   Better a live sinner than a dead saint.

I am much worse than people think I am, and also much better.

*Aphorism*

One cannot be what one should be merely by closing one's eyes to what one is.

*Aphorism*

Sometimes we think we are being patient when we are only being persistent.

*Aphorism*

To a truly honest man, it is a source of no satisfaction whatever to be credited with successes he has not achieved or virtues he does not possess.

*Aphorism*

You can only lead a simple life if you remember what life is really for. The purpose of simplicity is not to let the business of living get in the way of the things that are of importance.

*Seminar on The Door of Liberation*

Unless one solves the problem of Right Livelihood (or rather, the problem of wrong livelihood), to some extent at least, spiritual development can be quite difficult.

*Correspondence*

*Aphorism*  Hardly anybody is willing to give. Everybody wants to get. We search for someone without 'needs' so that we can obtain from him everything for nothing, as it were. Is this, perhaps, the reason why Gurdjieff insisted that everything must be paid for? Perhaps it is immoral to give something for nothing – one is encouraging greed and selfishness. At the time of Tantric initiation one has to make a cash payment to the guru. How much one is prepared to give shows how much – or how little – one values the initiation.

*Seminar on The Precious Garland*  Giving is the natural, unforced interchange of one's energy with that of others. In this sense real giving is receiving.

*Aphorism*  We should receive rather than take, give rather than impose, share rather than divide.

*Aphorism*  We often think that people are behaving most characteristically when they are behaving most badly. We often think the same thing about ourselves.

One should not waste time helping the weak. Nowadays it is the strong who need help.

*Aphorism*

There is no feeling of joy without a feeling of strength. The weak, therefore, cannot be joyful.

*Aphorism*

If we want a definition of Faith we may say that it is the response, even the emotional response, of what is ultimate in us to what is ultimate in the Universe.

*The Stages of the Spiritual Path. Lecture*

Faith is one's emotional response to something higher than oneself. And because it is higher one cannot possibly understand it.

*Seminar on The Door of Liberation*

Genuine devotion dissolves whatever is not genuine in the object of devotion. You can't be taken in, can't be deceived, if you enter into a situation with genuine feelings, with true integrity.

*ibid.*

Faith is innate, doubt acquired.

*Aphorism*

*Aphorism*    According to the *Abhidharma*, faith (*shraddha*) is present in all skilful mental states. Faith consists in being aware of, and responsive to, that which is higher. All skilful mental states are, therefore, essentially progressive. The terrifying corollary of this last fact is, of course, that all unskilful mental states have an inherent tendency to deteriorate, i.e. to become still more unskilful. There is never a state of perfect equilibrium between the skilful and the unskilful. One either ascends or descends in the scale of consciousness. Once one has passed the 'point of no return', however, there is only the possibility of ascent.

*Aphorism*    Monks should appear to come from another world, not just another country.

*Aphorism*    There are four kinds of disciples: disciples who are like patients; disciples who are like friends; disciples who are like sons; and disciples who are like lovers.

There is no question of our making sacred cows of anything, but rather of trying to develop a spirit of reverence.... One might go so far as to say that it is better to have sacred cows, even in the literal sense, than to hold nothing sacred.

*Correspondence*

Gurus are the middlemen of religion.

*Aphorism*

In all traditional civilizations the relation between master and disciple was one of the basic facts of life, and to be without a teacher was synonymous with being without education or culture of any kind.

*A Survey of Buddhism*

The good is very often the enemy of the best.

*Seminar on The Stability of Societies*

EMOTION & REASON

*The Path of the Inner Life*

THE EARLY STAGES of the career of a spiritual aspirant are a period of unceasing struggle between the lower and higher impulses of his nature. On the outcome of this struggle depends the success or failure of his vocation. If he is able to resist the solicitations of the objects of perception and turn his senses as it were inside out, like the five fingers of a glove, thus reversing their direction, they will merge into a single inner sense, and with this subtle inner sense he will be able to perceive spiritual realities.

*Seminar on The Buddha*

*The over-developed intellect and the under-developed emotions* – it's really a pathetic sort of combination; but most people have this combination in some degree, don't they? In your conscious mind you're a great big man, but unconsciously you're just a little child – possibly, in some cases, crying for mother – or even a baby just howling for the breast.

I was reading a book the other day which had a chapter    *ibid.*
called 'The Pathology of Thinking', and it said – and
this is one of the things that I've been saying lately –
that excessive thinking is pathological.

One of the ways in which one can counterbalance    *ibid.*
excessive thinking is through contact with Nature and
the elements. One can develop one's sense
consciousness (for want of a better term) by contact with
earth, fire, water, space – it's as simple as that. This will
take a lot of the tension and one-sidedness out of one's
mental development, and out of one's will.

# REMEMBERING THE RETREAT

At the wood's edge, a solitary hut;
Sharing my quiet room, a single friend.
Here on the table, two or three books of verse;
There on the shelf, half a dozen frost-blackened violets. Hour
after hour, we exchange only a few words;
Day after day, I polish a single poem.
Who would have thought it? A whole world of content
Found in these things!

If your emotions are here and your reason as it were there, then it's a question of being guided either by your reason or by your emotions – which means you're not an integrated person. The integrated person acts as a total person. There is emotionality in what he does, and also reason – meaning a sort of aware recognition of certain objective facts and circumstances and possibilities.

*Seminar on the Ratnaguna-Samchayagatha*

When we are totally integrated, and our reason is our emotion and our emotion our reason, it's quite difficult for us to say, sometimes, whether we do things on account of certain reasons or just because we feel like doing them. We have become as it were one: one whole.

*ibid.*

It is very important to develop a very positive emotional counterpart to one's intellectual understanding, and this is where the development of *maitri, karuna, mudita, upeksha*[3] – to say nothing of faith and devotion – comes in.

*Seminar on The Buddha*

*ibid.*   Inasmuch as our emergence as individuals, or at least [as] the beginnings of individuals, has been via the development of independent thinking, we have above all else to be on the look-out that our one-sided thinking doesn't develop too disproportionately, and that we give a great deal of attention to the development of all the other sides of ourselves, especially the emotional: that we reinforce that as much as possible and lift our emotions to a correspondingly high level. Otherwise there will be no development, no emergence of true individuality. We shall all have dragons' heads and snakes' bodies.

*Seminar on Outlines of Mahayana Buddhism*   It seems to me that the strength of the Tantric tradition, the Vajrayana[11] tradition, Tibetan Buddhism generally, is the presence in it of symbols. But it seems that in Japanese Buddhism, at least as presented by Suzuki and others, you've got philosophy on the one hand and emotion on the other, and what should be symbols, traditionally, have become converted simply into objects of emotion. So there's no unification taking place.

Seeing is active, hearing is passive. When one visualizes the form of a Buddha or Bodhisattva, and hears the sound of his mantra, one is being simultaneously active and passive, 'masculine' and 'feminine'.

*Aphorism*

When you start thinking, you start thinking of what is possible. But the mere fact that it is possible does not mean that it is desirable. When you develop, or over-develop, the thinking faculty, you tend to think that because you can *think* of doing something, that is sufficient reason for doing it. In this way, imbalance develops. A very good example of this in modern times is the space programme. It's as though, if you can think of doing something, you should do it. But the capacity for abstract thinking runs far ahead of the development, or even the needs, of the organism as a whole.

*Seminar on The Buddha*

Opposites are not to be eliminated, but reconciled within a higher unity.

*Aphorism*

# THE INDIVIDUAL

*A System of*
*Meditation. Lecture*

TO BEGIN WITH, when we come – I might even say, staggering – along to our first meditation class, maybe from the office, from home, or wheresoever, we don't have any real individuality. We are usually just a bundle of conflicting desires and selves, both conscious and unconscious, loosely tied together with the thread of a name and address! When we practise Mindfulness of Breathing, it helps bring them together; it at least tightens the string a little bit so that they aren't so loose in the middle; it makes of these different cravings and selves more of a definite, recognizable, identifiable bundle.

In the individual, when you force your organism to go along in accordance with something that you've merely thought, *because* you've thought it, then there's great strain on the organism. And this is the nature of mind; this is the nature of rational thinking. So inasmuch as it is through rational thinking that the individual begins to be emancipated from the group, the person who is emancipated from the group is, to begin with, an *unbalanced* person, a person whose thinking is in excess of his emotional development and so on. That is individualism. To become an individual, what you have to do is to restrain your one-sided intellectual development and cultivate your emotional side, and thus develop as an individual in a more integrated way – on a higher level, on a more conscious level – than the primitive member of the tribe. Once you've achieved that more all-round development which is covered in Buddhist teaching by the teaching of the Five Spiritual Faculties – then you can go on to develop your true individuality.

*Seminar on The Buddha*

# SCAPEGOAT

How did it feel
To be left alone in the desert
Loaded down with the sins
Of a whole people?

How did it feel
To have hanging round your neck
Dragging on your horns clogging
Your steps thousands of
Thefts murders fornications
Perjuries blasphemies –
Sins of a whole people
For a whole year?
How did it feel
To be weighed down by all that,
You just a black goat,
Comparatively small?

Vultures circling
Overhead, did you remember
Hands of the High Priest on your head, flash
Of the jewels on his breastplate, remember
The last shouts dying behind you
As you were left alone in the desert
Crushed beneath the weight of the sins
Of a whole people?

How did it feel?

Not so bad, I think,
As being left alone in the universe
With one's *own* guilt.

Mankind should be grateful
To goats.

*A System of*
*Meditation. Lecture*

You can't commit yourself unless there is just one individuality to commit itself.

*Aphorism*

Because one is in a minority of one, it does not necessarily follow that one is more of an individual.

*Seminar on The*
*Buddha*

When we speak of the emergence of the individual from the group, we are not to think of an all-round-developed individual emerging from the group. It doesn't seem to happen that way. What happens is that, usually, emancipation from the group occurs via the intellect, via the development of independent thinking, and that, therefore, what emerges is an unbalanced person, a one-sidedly developed person, and that one-sidedly developed person we still have very much with us. Therefore one of the most pressing tasks, within the context of individual development, is to bring the emotions up into harmony with the intellect, and have a more all-round development.

Having prised yourself free from the group and the group consciousness, to some extent, by means of your developed intelligence, you haven't got to continue developing just your intelligence more and more – you've almost got to stop developing your intelligence (that's developed sufficiently for the time being) and develop the rest of you and achieve a sort of *emotional* independence of the tribe: a development of emotion as a true individual.

*ibid.*

It is usually your thinking faculty which is the means of your emancipation from the group, but, because it is on account of the over-development of the thinking faculty that you've emancipated yourself from the group, when you are emancipated, or at least to some extent emancipated, you find yourself a one-sidedly developed person. And very often you find yourself in a situation of conflict, because mentally you have emancipated from the group, but emotionally, to a great extent, you still belong to it!

*Seminar on The Buddha*

*ibid.*   Nowadays we've got quite a lot of individualists: people
who are mentally emancipated from the group, though
still belonging to it emotionally; people who are capable
of a great deal of mental activity, and who sometimes try
to gear the whole of their being to the purely one-sided
ideals of that over-developed intellect. But it would
seem that this is a necessary stage of development.

*ibid.*   *Q.* You say that it's a necessary intermediate step. Can't
you go straight to work on your emotions without going
through this intellectual phase?
*A.* It would seem not. I don't say that you can't. I mean,
if you've got favourable conditions, yes, I think you
could; but in the modern world those favourable
conditions hardly ever exist.

*ibid.*   It is, in a way, a necessary process. For most people, to
develop in any other way is difficult. They start thinking
independently usually before they become independent
in any other way.

The teaching of the Buddha was concerned with the *ibid.*
development of the individual. Admittedly that
development had, through ethics, a social dimension, but
the Buddha was not concerned with 'something much
wider, the whole realm of sentient Being' in opposition,
as it were, to the individual. He was not concerned with
the development of the group as such, or the well-being
of the group as such: he was concerned with the
development of individuals *as* individuals.

Every true individual is a whole species in himself. *Aphorism*

Individuals are incommensurable. *Aphorism*

One can legislate for the group, but not for the *Aphorism*
individual.

One can generalize about people only to the extent that *Aphorism*
they are not individuals.

*Aphorism* Jewels are produced only by the collision of immense forces.

*The Individual, the Group, and the Spiritual Community. Lecture* Truth is more likely to be with the individual than with the group.

*ibid.* The group is always wrong.

TEACHING & STUDY

*Correspondence*  WHAT IS NEEDED so far as [real help in the actual spiritual development of the individual] is concerned is not books, but the living context of a spiritual fellowship and concrete spiritual teachings appropriate to one's actual requirements. In other words, there is a great deal that we do not need to know, that we can safely ignore. Then why is it that we go on reading? Only too often, I suspect, it is because reading, including the reading of religious literature, has become a form of mental distraction. However, if even the reading of good religious books does not help us much, what is one to say of the reading of bad books – books which are the product of ill-digested information, muddled thinking, unconscious rationalization, and downright spiritual delusion and confusion? And such books are in the majority.

*Seminar on The Door of Liberation*  There is a great deal to be said for a thorough knowledge of a small number of works, rather than a superficial knowledge of many.

Many years ago, I constantly asked myself: 'How does this teaching relate to one's actual spiritual experience, spiritual life, and spiritual development? Why did the Buddha say this? Why was the Buddha concerned with this? Where does it connect up with spiritual life?' And I found that very, very few scholars ever thought in those terms. In many cases it didn't even seem to occur to them to do so – even to Buddhists themselves, very often. As though it was just a sort of game, you know, that had no relevance to life and no bearing on the spiritual life or on spiritual development as an individual.

*Seminar on The Buddha*

It is fashionable among some modern 'intellectuals' to run down the intellect. In this way they seek to give the impression that they have transcended its limitations. However, their understanding of the limitations of the intellect remains – purely intellectual.

*ibid.*

To people immersed in worldly states of mind, the Dharma[12] will inevitably appear negative because it opposes what they have based their lives on.

*Seminar on The Door of Liberation*

*Seminar on The Buddha*  Only from the intellectual or dogmatic scientific point of view is it possible to regard Buddhism as being merely one among hundreds of other possible subjects of scholarly research and doctoral dissertation. To one who studies it with some attempt at approximation to the fully traditional method ... it can appear as nothing less than what it actually is, the dominating and controlling influence of the whole of life.

*ibid.*  The quest for holiness, which the study of the Dharma subserves, is a quest for spiritual wholeness, for complete integration of the 'personality' not with any subjective principle merely, but with Reality.

*Aphorism*  The Dharma is the Buddha's Enlightenment objectified, and therefore falsified.

*Correspondence*  The more committed should *help* the less committed rather than feel impatient with them; the less committed should *revere* the more committed and be grateful to them, rather than feel inferior and resentful.

One is able to communicate the Dharma, through any *ibid.*
medium, only to the extent that one has realized it in
one's own heart and mind, one's own life. Realization of
the Dharma must therefore logically – and spiritually –
precede the expression and communication of the
Dharma. This is not to say that only a fully enlightened
being is able to teach, but simply that before
communicating one must have something to
communicate, even though one discovers what that is
only in the process of communication.

One of the biggest sources of confusion and *ibid.*
misunderstanding here in the West, so far as Buddhism
is concerned, is that we have talked in terms of 'monks',
'monasteries', etc., which gives a totally wrong
impression of the Buddhist spiritual life. I really do wish
we could get rid of all these terms once and for all –
including the word 'religion'.

We are usually able to bear much more than we – and *ibid.*
others – think we can.

*ibid.*  People should be encouraged to rely on themselves to the extent that they are really *able* to rely on themselves. But it is no use expecting the baby to walk on his own two feet before his limbs are strong enough to support his body. It is the same with psychological and spiritual babies as with physical ones. Mother must not get impatient. Help and encourage them to grow up, by all means, but don't try to thrust independence on people who are not ready for it and who need, in fact, a further period of 'dependence' (perhaps 'apprenticeship' would be a better word) before being in a position to set up on their own.

*ibid.*  If we could only *realize* a hundredth part of what we *understand* we should all become Buddhas on the spot.

*Seminar on The Door of Liberation*  One can only speak the truth to one person. The larger the number of people to whom you are speaking, the more will what you say become an approximation to the truth.

An academic is not an intellectual. An intellectual has a *ibid.*
strong creative element in his thought.

Theology is to mysticism as literary criticism is to poetry. *Aphorism*

Philosophy is the rational construction of reality. *Aphorism*

Genuine emotional involvement in the spiritual life, as *Correspondence*
distinct from the initial sensation of excitement and
discovery, usually requires much more time for its
development than intellectual involvement.

The Higher Evolution consists in the conscious *Aphorism*
acceptance of the action of the Absolute upon oneself
and others.

The teachings contained in the *Dhammapada*[13] are literal *Aphorism*
truth, and deserve to be engraved on our hearts in letters
of gold – or fire.

# HOMAGE TO WILLIAM BLAKE

My Spectre stands there white as snow;
Whate'er I ask, he answers 'No'.
Till I can melt him with my fire
He blocks the path of my desire.

My Emanation, weak and poor,
Lies outstretched upon the floor.
Till I can claim her for my own
Both of us must howl and groan.

Therefore will I, all I can,
Build up complete the Fourfold Man,
Head and heart, and loins fine,
And hands and feet, all made divine.

Banish single vision far!
With double vision ever war!
Fourfold vision night and day
Light and guide you on your way.

In that fourfold vision bright
See the whole world with delight.
Rock and stone, and flower and tree,
And bird and beast, are men like thee.

Men like thee, and women too,
Androgynous, ever-new –
Divine Imaginations free
Exulting in Eternity.

*Aphorism*   Commentary must itself be creation, or it is not even commentary.

*Aphorism*   The truth does not scorch you nearly as fiercely as the suffering you bring upon yourself when you ignore the truth.

*Aphorism*   The Buddha taught and influenced people by what he was, far more than by what he said.

# MEDITATION

*Seminar on The
Door of Liberation*

MEDITATION IS the uninterrupted production of skilful mental states.

*The Stages of the
Spiritual Path.
Lecture*

When we are completely happy, and all our emotional energies are unified, then we are concentrated, in the true sense. Hence we may say that a concentrated person is a happy person, a happy person is a concentrated person, and the happier we are, the longer we shall be able to stay concentrated. We find it difficult to stay concentrated for very long because we are not happy with our present state. If we were really and truly happy we wouldn't need to do anything else: we would just stay still enjoying that happiness. But we are not happy, we are dissatisfied, and so we get restless, and go searching for this, searching for that – for some distraction, some diversion – and in this way there is no concentration.

*Seminar on
Dhyana for
Beginners*

Sloth is the weight of one's actual existence resisting further evolving.

In the period of sleep, one's mindfulness is impeded. Meditation helps one to maintain the creativity of the dream state into waking life, blending the richness of dream state with the clarity of the waking state.

*Seminar on The Door of Liberation*

In a sleep you come to the class, in a sleep you listen to the lecture, in a sleep even you meditate.... You may not actually be dead but all these activities are carried on in sleep.

*Meditation: the Expanding Consciousness. Lecture*

Concentration ... is a union, or a marriage if you like, of the forces of the depths with the forces of the heights.

*ibid.*

Heaven, the ultimate goal of so many faiths, since it is a mode of contingent and hence of transitory existence, is accounted no more than a pleasant interlude in a pilgrimage fundamentally of more serious import.

*The Three Jewels*

The object of meditation is to transform oneself, not to have good meditations.

*Aphorism*

*A System of*
*Meditation. Lecture*

The Four Superconscious States, the four so-called lower *dhyanas*, are within the reach of everybody who meditates systematically and regularly.

*Aphorism*

A *dhyana* is not a 'state' in which 'we' are, but a way in which we reorganize our being.

*The Path of*
*Regular and the*
*Path of Irregular*
*Steps. Lecture*

When one mentions 'Meditation without Any Steps At All' one at once finds people becoming rather interested. They're not at all interested in 'Meditation by Regular Steps': *that* sounds rather dull, rather prosaic. 'Meditation by Irregular Steps' appeals to them quite a bit, but what *really* captivates and fascinates them is this idea of 'Meditation with No Steps At All'!… Unfortunately the attraction is usually entirely for the wrong reasons!

*A System of*
*Meditation. Lecture*

*Shunyata*[14] could well be rendered 'Death' because it is the death of everything conditioned, and it is only when the conditioned individuality dies that the unconditioned individuality begins to emerge.

To state the matter axiomatically, we may say that a higher stage of the Path cannot be developed in its fullness, or even to a moderate extent, before a lower stage of the Path has been developed in its fullness. This is the basic principle.

*The Path of Regular and the Path of Irregular Steps. Lecture*

In meditation, as we go deeper and deeper, we often experience a great fear. Sometimes people shy away from this fear, but it is good to allow oneself to experience it. That fear occurs when we feel what may be called 'the touch of *shunyata*', the touch of Reality, on the conditioned self. And the touch of Reality on the conditioned self feels like death. It *is* death, for the conditioned self, so the conditioned self feels afraid.

*A System of Meditation. Lecture*

It would appear that, for some people at least, the experience of causeless, nameless fear, often prolonged, and of great intensity, is a necessary part of the process of spiritual self-development. But the function of experience, however dreadful, is positive. Indeed one might say, the more dreadful, the more positive.

*Correspondence*

*A System of*
*Meditation. Lecture*

*Shamatha*[15] develops and refines our conditioned individuality; *vipashyana*[16] breaks down that individual: enables us to see right through it.

*Aphorism*

To say that matter is evil is to say that it is not material.

*The Three Jewels*

For Buddhism, no less than for modern physics and psychology, all the apparently stable and solid material and mental objects in the universe are in reality temporary condensations of energy. Hence despite what some have assumed the use of such words as 'states' and 'elements' to mean, seeing conditioned things as impermanent does not consist in conceiving them as chopped up into bits (which would raise the artificial problem of how the bits were to be joined together again), but rather in seeing them as so many phases of one or the other of two pure, absolutely continuous, interdependent streams of energy which can be locked up in the atom, in the one case, and trapped in the individual mind, in the other.

We swivel round and round in time on the pivot of
eternity.

*Aphorism*

True, time is short; but that is no reason for being in a
hurry.

*Aphorism*

Time is part of our structure of consciousness.

*Seminar on The
Door of Liberation*

Time, like space, is curved. To go forwards in time is,
therefore, to go backwards, and vice versa.

*Aphorism*

The true Esoteric Path, the true Secret Teaching, the true
Doctrine of the Heart, the true Master, is not to be found
in any book, or, indeed, anywhere at all in the outside
world, but in the heart-depths of the spiritual experience
of the individual devotee.

*The Path of the
Inner Life*

There is no infallible criterion by means of which the
unenlightened can recognize the Enlightened.

*Aphorism*

*The Path of the Inner Life*   Any practice which heightens one's ego-sense, however holy in popular estimation it may be, is unspiritual, and any practice which attenuates it, however mean and despicable outwardly it may seem, is spiritual in the truest and best sense of the term.

*A System of Meditation. Lecture*   The figure of a Bodhisattva, sublime and glorious though it may be, is, in fact, you – is the new you – you as you will be if only you allow yourself to die.

*ibid.*   Death is a state of enforced meditation.

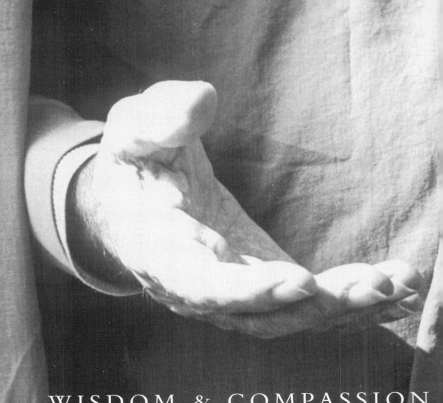

WISDOM & COMPASSION

*The Path of the*
*Inner Life*

EVERY SINGLE THING in the universe, however mean or insignificant it may outwardly seem, bears deep within itself … the trace of absolute purity and perfection. This is the famous Jewel which the great Sanskrit mantra *om mani padme hum*, so beloved of the people of Tibet, informs us lies hidden in what is, microcosmically speaking, the heart-lotus of every being, and what is, macrocosmically speaking, the world-lotus of mundane existence itself.

Thus it is possible to analyse every single object in the universe into an Absolute, nirvanic, or perfect aspect, and a relative, samsaric, and imperfect aspect. In Tantric Buddhism the former is often spoken of as the vajra or diamond aspect of existence. Everything possesses a diamond or noumenal aspect corresponding to its material or phenomenal aspect. Corresponding to the simple earthly flower springing up from the soil there is a transcendental Diamond Flower, which is that aspect of the flower in which it is perfumed by, or in which it reflects and is reflected by, the reality of Suchness.[17] Similarly, as the transcendental aspect of our fickle and unsteady mundane mind there exists the mind which is 'pure and hard as flaming diamond', the Vajrachitta – human personality in its highest possible aspect of freeness, mutuality, and interpenetratingness with regard to all other things in the universe. That highest and most real aspect of existence in which everything interpenetrates every other thing, and wherein everything reflects, and is in turn reflected by, every other phenomenon (offering no obstruction to each other whatsoever, like the mutual interpenetration of innumerable beams of coloured light) is called the *Dharmadhatu*, the Realm of Truth, or the *Vajradhatu*, the Diamond World. The Bodhisattva aspires to live in this world, the world of realities, instead of in that presented by the ordinary mundane consciousness, the world of illusions.

The activity of emptiness is compassion. *ibid.*

We purify ourselves truly by waking up to the fact that we have never become impure. *Aphorism*

*The Path of the Inner Life* Since the Path of the Inner Life consists essentially in a series of experiences, and since all experiences are by their very nature ineffable, it is also an Esoteric as opposed to an Exoteric Path. Nothing in the religious life is truly esoteric save spiritual experience. The most private ritual, the abstrusest philosophical doctrine, the most jealously guarded scripture, the most secret society or organization, are all exoteric. They belong to the domain of 'Head-learning' rather than to the domain of 'Soul-wisdom', and, as *The Voice of the Silence* emphatically admonishes us, it is above all things necessary to learn to separate the one from the other, to learn to discriminate between 'The Doctrine of the Eye' and 'The Doctrine of the Heart'.

*ibid.* The individual self is a centre from which all lines of discrimination radiate in all directions. It is the innermost citadel of separateness. Only when this centre expands to infinity, only when the walls of this citadel are razed to the ground, is the consummation of the spiritual life achieved.

One is pure from the beginning; pure, if you like, from the beginningless beginning; pure by nature; pure essentially. For anyone brought up in a guilt-ridden culture like ours in the West, this sort of statement must surely come as a great positive shock: that in the depths of your being you are pure of all conditionality; pure of the very distinction between conditioned and unconditioned, and hence you are Void.

*ibid.*

We have the potentiality; if we make the effort we can get there [Enlightenment]. But we are not destined in the sense that we *must* gain Enlightenment, whether we like it or not, as it were! No. The *samsara*[18] can go on and on indefinitely. You can remain in it indefinitely. You can remain indefinitely unenlightened and go on, you know, to eternity, as it were. You are not 'destined' for Enlightenment! *You don't have to have Enlightenment if you don't want it!*

*Seminar on Outlines of Mahayana Buddhism*

No accumulation of karma[19] can get you to nirvana.[20]

*ibid.*

*The Three Jewels*   According to Buddhism a man is not, strictly speaking, reborn as an animal, neither is he reborn as a man, nor as a god. What is 'reborn', in the sense of becoming temporarily linked to an appropriate form, is the continuously changing stream of psychical energy.

*ibid.*   Energy is primary, form secondary. It is not that man wills, but rather that will 'mans'.

*The Three Jewels*   To dedicate oneself to the salvation of others with the conviction that there in reality exist others who need saving is as much a source of bondage as to devote oneself to the task of one's own liberation under the impression that one has a real self to be liberated.

*Aphorism*   One does not feel compassion for beings because they suffer. One simply feels compassion.

*Aphorism*   A tiny speck of dust in the eye can prevent one from seeing. A single misunderstanding can obstruct one's vision of the Truth.

Purity is power.

*Aphorism*

The one root-illusion which prevents us from seeing things as they really are, and which it is the primary business of spiritual practice to remove, is the belief in ourselves as separate, perduring individual selves or ego-entities.

*The Path of the Inner Life*

When we see that the Path of the Inner Life, the true Esoteric Path, the Way of Emptiness and the Way of Compassion, and the Middle Way, are all aspects of the One Way, the Way taught by the Buddha, we begin to glimpse the profound truth of the saying that 'The Path is one for all, the means to reach the goal must vary with the Pilgrims.'

*ibid.*

I have no before or after, neither beginning nor end.

*Aphorism*

Growth in holiness is essentially growth in emptiness.

*The Path of the Inner Life*

*ibid.*   He who conceives the spiritual life as a means of attaining eternal bliss has not understood. The whole conception of attainment is fundamentally wrong. One has simply to break down the barriers of his separative individuality and allow himself to be penetrated by everything that exists. Then he will himself penetrate everything. This mutual penetration is liberation, is happiness.

*Seminar on The Door of Liberation*   The culmination of wisdom is freedom from all views. You have nothing to say. When all the answers are in your being, you have no need to keep them in your head.

*Aphorism*   Peace is a fire.

# NOTES

1 The three *lakshanas* are the 'characteristics' or 'marks' of conditioned existence: *anitya* or 'impermanence', *anatman* or 'insubstantiality', and thirdly *duhkha*: 'suffering' or 'unsatisfactoriness'.

2 Members of the Western Buddhist Order undertake to apply ten principles of spiritual development traditionally known as 'precepts' (*sikshapada*).

3 These are the *brahma viharas* or positive emotions of friendliness (*maitri*, Pali *metta*), compassion (*karuna*), sympathetic joy (*mudita*), and equanimity (*upeksha*, Pali *upekkha*), all of which have to be developed to a limitless extent.

4 The Three Jewels, so called because they represent the highest values in Buddhism, are the *Buddha*, the personified spiritual ideal, the *Dharma*, the teaching of the Way to the realization of the spiritual ideal, and the *Sangha*, the community of those following the Way.

5 *Bodhisattva*, literally 'Enlightenment-being'. Someone committed to the attainment of Perfect Enlightenment for the sake of all living beings.

6 *Samvara*, literally 'binding'; commitment, ordination.

7 *Upasaka*, a lay devotee. At the time of this lecture, members of the Western Buddhist Order were styled *upasakas* (m.) and *upasikas* (f.), a traditional lay ordination. Because the lay–monastic division is not relevant to ordination within the WBO, this was later changed to *Dharmachari* (m.) and *Dharmacharini* (f.) (literally, 'Dharma-farer').

8 *Bhikshu* (Pali: *bhikkhu*), a Buddhist monk.

9 *Three Refuges*, the Three Jewels as objects of personal commitment.

10 *Mitra*, literally 'friend'. In the FWBO, one formally engaged in its teachings and activities as their personal spiritual path, and possibly thinking in terms of eventual ordination as a *Dharmachari* (see note 7).

11 *Vajrayana*, the 'Adamantine Way' or 'Diamond Path', the third phase of the historical development of Indian Buddhism.

12 *Dharma*, the Truth, the Buddha's teaching.

13 *Dhammapada*, an ancient and very popular Buddhist scripture, in its Pali form consisting of 423 verse aphorisms (*pada*) on the Buddha's Teaching (*Dhamma*).

14 *Shunyata*, literally 'Voidness' or 'Emptiness'; ultimate Reality.

15 *Shamatha*, literally 'calm'; the progressive unification of (mundane) consciousness.

16 *Vipashyana*, literally 'clear seeing'; insight into ultimate Reality.

17 *Suchness*, *tathata* or ultimate Reality.

18 *Samsara*, conditioned (mundane) existence; the process of repeated rebirth.

19 *Karma*, literally 'action', good action or merit.

20 *Nirvana*, the goal of Buddhism.

# SOURCES

## Seminars by Sangharakshita:

Unpublished seminar on *The Buddha* by Trevor Ling (Pelican 1976)

Unpublished seminar on 'Dhyana for Beginners' in *A Buddhist Bible* ed. D. Goddard (Beacon, Boston 1970)

Unpublished seminar on *The Door of Liberation* by Geshe Wangyal (Maurice Girodias, New York 1973)

Unpublished seminar on *Outlines of Mahayana Buddhism* by D.T. Suzuki (Rider, London 1963)

Unpublished seminar on *The Precious Garland* by Nagarjuna, trans. and ed. J. Hopkins and Lati Rimpoche (Allen and Unwin, London 1975)

Seminar on the *Ratnaguna-Samchayagatha*, published (in part) in *Wisdom Beyond Words*, Windhorse, 1993

Seminar on the *Sutta-Nipata*, extract published in *Mitrata* No.2 (revised edition)

Seminar on 'The Stability of Societies' based on *Some Sayings of the Buddha*, trans. F.L. Woodward (OUP 1973). Extract published in *Mitrata* No.2 (revised edition)

LECTURES BY SANGHARAKSHITA:

'Art and Spiritual Life' London 1969, Dharmachakra Tape no.77

'Breaking through to Buddhahood' London 1969, Dharmachakra Tape no.63

'The Essence of Zen' 1965, Dharmachakra Tapes nos.13–16 (published)

'The Individual, the Group, and the Spiritual Community' London 1971, Dharmachakra Tape no.91

'Meditation: the Expanding Consciousness' London 1967, Dharmachakra Tape no.33

'A Method of Personal Development' Brighton 1976, Dharmachakra Tape no.131

'Mind Reactive and Creative' 1967, Dharmachakra Tape no.31 (published)

'The Path of Regular and the Path of Irregular Steps' London 1974, Dharmachakra Tape no.118

'The Stages of the Spiritual Path' Bristol 1967, Dharmachakra Tape no.34

'A System of Meditation' Fourth Convention of the Western Buddhist Order, 1978, Dharmachakra Tape no.135

Taped lectures are available from

DHARMACHAKRA TAPES, P.O. BOX 50, CAMBRIDGE, CB1 3BG

ESSAYS BY SANGHARAKSHITA:

'Buddhism and Art', Maha Bodhi Society of Kalimpong, 1956
'Buddhism and William Blake', *Fwbo Newsletter 36*, FWBO 1977
'The Path of the Inner Life', in *Crossing the Stream*, Windhorse 1987

BOOKS BY SANGHARAKSHITA:

*The Essence of Zen*, Windhorse 1992
*Mind Reactive and Creative*, Windhorse 1989
*The Religion of Art*, Windhorse 1988
*A Survey of Buddhism*, Windhorse 1993
*The Three Jewels: An Introduction to Buddhism*, Windhorse 1991

The above are available from:

WINDHORSE PUBLICATIONS
UNIT 1-316 THE CUSTARD FACTORY
GIBB STREET
BIRMINGHAM
B9 4AA
UK

ARYALOKA
HEARTWOOD CIRCLE
NEWMARKET
NEW HAMPSHIRE
NH 03857
USA

# ILLUSTRATIONS

All photographs © the Clear Vision Trust Picture Archive.
Details of some of the photographs are given below

The Windhorse symbolizes the energy of the enlightened mind carrying the Three Jewels – the Buddha, the Dharma, and the Sangha – to all sentient beings.

Buddhism is one of the fastest growing spiritual traditions in the Western world. Throughout its 2,500-year history, it has always succeeded in adapting its mode of expression to suit whatever culture it has encountered.

Windhorse Publications aims to continue this tradition as Buddhism comes to the West. Today's Westerners are heirs to the entire Buddhist tradition, free to draw instruction and inspiration from all the many schools and branches. Windhorse publishes works by authors who not only understand the Buddhist tradition but are also familiar with Western culture and the Western mind.

For orders and catalogues contact

WINDHORSE PUBLICATIONS
UNIT 1-316 THE CUSTARD FACTORY
GIBB STREET
BIRMINGHAM
B9 4AA
UK

ARYALOKA
HEARTWOOD CIRCLE
NEWMARKET
NEW HAMPSHIRE
NH 03857
USA

Windhorse Publications is an arm of the Friends of the Western Buddhist Order, which has more than forty centres on four continents. Through these centres, members of the Western Buddhist Order offer regular programmes of events for the general public and for more experienced students. These include meditation classes, public talks, study on Buddhist themes and texts, and 'bodywork' classes such as t'ai chi, yoga, and massage. The FWBO also runs several retreat centres and the Karuna Trust, a fundraising charity that supports social welfare projects in the slums and villages of India.

Many FWBO centres have residential spiritual communities and ethical businesses associated with them. Arts activities are encouraged too, as is the development of strong bonds of friendship between people who share the same ideals. In this way the FWBO is developing a unique approach to Buddhism, not simply as a set of techniques, less still as an exotic cultural interest, but as a creatively directed way of life for people living in the modern world.

If you would like more information about the FWBO please write to the

LONDON BUDDHIST CENTRE          ARYALOKA
51 ROMAN ROAD                   HEARTWOOD CIRCLE
LONDON                          NEWMARKET
E2 0HU                          NH 03857
UK                              USA

# ALSO FROM WINDHORSE

SUBHUTI
SANGHARAKSHITA:
A NEW VOICE IN THE BUDDHIST TRADITION

Sangharakshita has established one of the most successful Buddhist movements in the modern world. And yet he is regarded even now in some quarters as a controversial figure. Unafraid to communicate strongly held views and insights, even when they challenge long-venerated elements of Buddhist tradition, he has founded a new Buddhist Order whose male and female members are pioneering a 'living Buddhism' that seems ideally suited to our times.

   Here one of Sangharakshita's closest disciples, a respected writer in his own right, offers a comprehensive account of Sangharakshita's evolution as a thinker and teacher.

*336 pages*
*bibliography, index*
*£9.99/$19.95*

SANGHARAKSHITA
## THE TEN PILLARS OF BUDDHISM

The Ten Pillars of Buddhism are ten ethical principles, or precepts, which together provide a comprehensive guide to the moral dimension of life. To explore them is to turn the lens of moral vision on to every aspect of our lives. To apply them is to accept the challenge of human potential for higher development – and to work with that challenge in the arena of everyday activity.

All readers, Buddhist or not, will find this book a source of inspiration and insight in their quest for ethical standards by which to live.

*128 pages*
*ISBN 0-904766-39-X*
*£4.50/$8.95*

Sangharakshita
## A Guide to the Buddhist Path

Which teachings really matter? How does one begin to practise Buddhism in a systematic way? This is confusing territory. Without a guide one can get easily dispirited or lost.

Like all good guides, Sangharakshita knows the terrain extremely well. At the outset he steers us away from the dangers of sectarianism, the dangers of mistaking the part for the whole. He sorts out fact from myth, essence from cultural accident, to reveal the fundamental teachings of Buddhism.

*256 pages, illustrated, bibliography, index*
*ISBN 0-904766-35-7*
*£10.95/$21.95*

SANGHARAKSHITA
## CONQUERING NEW WORLDS: SELECTED POEMS

The poems range over a variety of topics, from a handful of wild orchids, and a mythical beast called the Windhorse, to the heroism of a Tibetan refugee. Sangharakshita presents this diversity of themes with a rich modulation of verse forms.

*64 pages*
*ISBN 0-904766-26-8*
*£3.95/$795*

KAMALASHILA
## MEDITATION: THE BUDDHIST WAY OF TRANQUILLITY AND INSIGHT

A comprehensive guide to the methods and theory of Buddhist meditation – what it is and where it might take us.

Written in an informal, accessible style, this book provides a complete introduction to the basic techniques for the novice, as well as detailed advice for more experienced meditators seeking to deepen their practice.

*288 pages*
*illustrated, index*
*ISBN 0-904766-56-X*
*£11.99/$22.99*